FORBIDDEN GOLF FROM COMMUNIST POLAND TO PGA PRO

FORBIDDEN GOLF FROM COMMUNIST POLAND TO PGA PRO

FINDING YOUR BEST GAME!

JERRY CHYLKOWSKI, PGA

One Path Press

ISBN 9798987135198

Cover design by: Lisa Krasnow
Photography by: David Emberling
Library of Congress Control Number: 2023902587
Printed in the United States of America

For my wife, for all the sacrifices she made to further my goals

"Golf is the closest game to the game we call life. You get bad breaks from good shots; you get good breaks from bad shots – but you have to play the ball where it lies."

– Bobby Jones

CONTENTS

PREFACE

"Nobody asked how you looked, just what you shot."
  – Sam Snead

I began my path to golf in 1998 when a friend who had hired me to work in his restaurant invited me to play golf with him. Work, for me, in the United States started the day I received my temporary work permit. Coming from communist Poland where I was forced to study Russian in school, I did not know any English, so working as a computer technician as I had been trained was out of the question. I was happy to wash dishes and at least make some money until I could sort things out, but his invitation to play golf that morning profoundly changed my life.

This book is about my own unique method of teaching and helping golfers of all levels improve their game. Discovering golf, learning the game, and developing this method of teaching was my path to playing golf. But in another sense my personal path to golf was coming from communist Poland to the Orange Hills Country Club in Connecticut, playing for the first time, and going on to become a PGA Professional later in life. I feel strongly, that as everyone's life is unique, everyone's physical structure and ability is unique, and so is their path to learning, playing, and enjoying golf.

The teaching philosophy discussed in this book revolves around the idea that my path to learning the game is not the same as your path. The perfect swing is not perfect if it fits my body and not yours. Often, I talk with golfers who love the game but are disheartened by a failure to progress. In fact, many golfers see their game falling apart rather than improving and, of course, this is incredibly frustrating, to the point where some talk about giving up the game altogether. That is why I started seriously looking at the way golfers grip the club, their balance, and the way they swing. The more lessons I taught the more I realized that treating everyone the same, giving them the same tools, was not going to work.

My approach is a little different. I focus on the individual's biomechanics. The chapters in this book appear in the order that I usually organize my lessons. Students begin by warming up. Then I evaluate their current skill level. Next, we set a goal together. Typically, I start with the shortest swing—putting— and graduate to longer and longer swings such as chipping, pitching, and full swing. Finally, we work on specialty shots and golf course management.

Often a small fix will cause a chain reaction and improve the swing without making drastic changes. But if you are a person who has taken lessons for years and has seen little to no improvement, or if you are someone who consistently improves just a little and then falls back doing the same thing over and over and expecting a different outcome, this is an example of the famous quote often misattributed to Albert Einstein, "The definition of insanity..." While I don't recommend jumping from one instructor to another, there comes a point where you need to look for a different approach.

In general, try to find the source of the problem that creates the chain reaction that causes inaccuracy. Once you find the main reason for things going wrong, other parts of the swing will often resolve themselves, and what remains to be corrected can be remedied more easily. Of course, there are no shortcuts, it does take a lot of work and practice to improve. However, by correcting your own unique shortcomings you will find you can advance faster and more steadily. Believe it or not, virtually anyone can improve their game given the right direction.

In addition to the practical advice I give, in each chapter I share a brief story about my personal journey to golf, my successes and failures. Some will decide to read this book cover to cover for entertainment value and for a full view of my approach to teaching. Others may cherry-pick my teaching tips from areas of personal concern. I do recommend that everyone read Chapter 2, "Your Grip," as it contains the essence of my particular method and I believe it can benefit almost any player. Choose your own path, skip the stories, and go straight to the meat of the lesson. This book can also be used as a reference to look back on because we all need to brush up from time to time. If you are not improving, you are falling back. Enjoy reading, and I hope whatever your path, you find something valuable to take with you. Happy golfing!

CHAPTER 1

WARM UP AND EVALUATE

A Hard Start in Communist Poland

"Practice yourself in little things, and thence proceed to greater."
-Epictetus

Having grown up in Torun, Poland, when I tell people where I am from the first thing they ask is, "Where is that?" I tell them it is where Nicolaus Copernicus, the famous astronomer and mathematician was born in 1473. The same Copernicus who formulated the idea that the earth rotates around the sun. While there is a golf course in Torun today called Tatford, the city I grew up in is still certainly not widely recognized in golf circles.

People are often surprised to find that I did not begin to play golf until years after I came to the United States at the age of thirty-seven. In fact, I had literally never even heard of the game until after I arrived in America at twenty-eight years of age. "How could anyone reach the age of twenty-eight never having heard of golf?" you might ask. The answer is simple. There was no golf in Poland when I lived there.

Communism had put an end to golf for fifty years following World War II. When the Communists took over Poland, golf became prohibited. The Communist party saw golf as emblematic of the upper class and so golf was outlawed until the advent of the workers' movement, called Solidarity, which culminated in 1989.

Television stations were state-owned, so the sport was not televised. It was, after all, forbidden. Anyway, very few families even owned TV sets. But as soon as I began to play golf, I knew it was "my game." Before my PGA training, I was completely self-taught. Yet, I was already winning some amateur Polish American Golf Association (PAGA) Tournaments.

As I later learned, once I had arrived in the United States, golf was played in Poland decades before World War II, and it is played there again today. Before WWII there were seven golf courses in Poland. The first was opened in 1906 and was recognized by the elite throughout Europe. One course called Szczawno Zdroj was on land taken over by Germany during the war. When the land was returned to Poland in 1945 it was no longer a functioning golf course.

There were rumours of a golf course that might have existed in Gdansk (one of Poland's famous seaside resorts), but there is no current proof that it ever did exist. In addition to these, there were a couple private courses and three fully functioning golf courses in Warsaw, Breslau (Wroclaw), and Posing (Poznan). These three courses were designed by Jules Laroche, Bernhard van Limburger, and Deni McIllroy, respectively.

During the 1990s golf was allowed to flourish again, and today there are about thirty-five courses in Poland. One of today's top clubs is Modry Las Golf Club. As yet, I have not had the pleasure of playing there. Modry Las was developed by Gary Player. This world-class course is characterized by distinct and dramatic bunkers. Modry Las put Poland on the world golfing map. It is located outside of Choszczno on the western side of Poland, near the Baltic Sea and the German border.

Sand Valley is another notable golf course in Poland today. In fact, the World Golf Awards recently named Sand Valley as the best golf course in Poland and one of the top 100 in Europe. If you play at Sand Valley, please let me know what you think.

Poland has even produced a few notable golfers. A strong amateur player and romantic figure in the early 1900s, Prince Karol Radziwill (not much information is available on Radziwill) and today's Adrian Meronk are among them.

Adrian Meronk is a Polish professional golfer who plays on the European Tour. He was born in Germany, but he is Polish. He played amateur golf in Poland as a child. He was ranked the number one player in 2011 according to the World Junior Golf Rankings. Then Adrian attended East Tennessee State where he distinguished himself by becoming the first Polish golfer to play the Palmer Cup. In the 2014–15 season he received All-American honors from PING and Golfweek. He totalled 29 rounds of par or better that season, including 4 rounds played in the 2019 Open de Portugal. In 2022 Meronk became the first Polish golfer ever to win a PGA Tournament.

Warm Up

As in any sport, it is important to warm up and to stretch before you start. I will point out the difference here between the two. Warming up is about getting your heart rate up and will actually raise your core temperature. A warm-up can be anything from an hour working out in the gym to a few simple exercises or even a brisk walk. After a warm-up you should feel more "awake" and focused. Stretching loosens your muscles to prevent injury and to increase your range of motion.

Since there are so many different exercises recommended for warming up and stretching in general, and specifically for golf, I won't go into them in detail. I will say, however, do not underestimate the importance of a general warm-up and of stretching. Make sure you develop your own regimen and feel ready to hit before you step up to the tee.

What I will be covering in this chapter is warming up your swing. Once you are ready to begin swinging, I recommend that you start with a wedge because it is the shortest club. The shortest club requires the least amount of stretching and impact on your body. Then work up to hitting with the longer clubs. Some people take a long time to warm up, others warm up more quickly. I tell my students to let me know when they feel comfortable to begin.

Evaluate

I always start by asking about any physical limitations that might affect my students' ability to play. This helps me to understand how I can help them. I cannot tell someone with a back injury to turn beyond their physical ability. It is only after learning about the player's level and physical abilities that I finally observe their swing.

As I observe the student's swing, I can see certain patterns. I pay special attention to the ball flight and body movement. I try to find the main source of the golfer's inconsistency. Lack of confidence in the golf swing is always connected to inconsistency. Many times, by eliminating the main source of inaccuracy, the whole swing can be improved.

I look for what is characteristic about their swing and ball flight. Is the golfer slicing (for right-handed, starting left and veering right) or hooking (starting right and veering left)? Some of my students tend to hook while the others have a tendency to slice. It is not often I find a player who consistently hits straight. But when I see that one ball goes to the right and one goes to the left, I know that person is manipulating their swing. It is very difficult to play consistently when you manipulate. I look at the grip. Does it fit the golfer's body? Bad posture comes with a bad grip. With the wrong grip the joints are fighting each other. A standard grip cannot be used for everyone. (Detailed information on correcting your grip is presented fully in Chapter 2.)

What I mean by manipulation is a forced or artificial change in the plane of the swing that does not flow naturally from the backswing to the moment of impact. Manipulation is a correction, an attempt to fix things midswing and change it so that the club face is square to the target at the moment of impact with the ball. It is common for instructors and golfers alike to try to fix a bad swing rather than to try to eliminate it. I always try to eliminate any and all manipulation from the swing.

With a complete beginner, I introduce the basic grip, posture, balance, and alignment. Usually, balance is not addressed in a golf lesson. However, balance is very important for consistency and should not be overlooked. One great thing about being a beginner is that there are no bad habits to break.

If you have played for a while the assessment phase is critical. Often a small adjustment can make a big difference in the entire game. I rarely ask long-time players to radically change their swing. It gives them too much to think about at one time and can have the opposite effect, causing confusion and making things worse.

You do not have to be very young or very flexible to begin

learning. Your journey can start at any time. What is most important is the joy you find in the learning process. For me, and I believe for most people, seeing improvement in their game is the most gratifying part of playing, no matter the level. Knowing that we are all different and come to the game with different backgrounds, strengths, and abilities is the cornerstone of my teaching method. This means assessing where you are and what needs to be adjusted to begin your journey toward your best game.

Set a Goal

It is important to have a goal in mind. It is hard to get anywhere when you don't know where you are trying to go. My goal has varied over the years. First it was to improve my accuracy. Then I worked on lowering my handicap further. And finally, I made the leap and decided to leave the security of a steady job and work toward becoming a PGA Professional. I have never regretted that decision.

Before I make any changes to my students' swing, I always ask if they want to tweak their game a little to have more fun and play socially with friends or do they want to really change their game and lower their handicap significantly. They need to think about how much effort they want to put into improvement, how much time they have available to practice. Also, whether they are willing to feel some awkwardness or discomfort in the beginning. Any change in a long-established golf swing will create some discomfort. Like many bad habits the old swing can be hard to break. It may feel strange or uncomfortable to hit the ball correctly until you get used to the feeling. Students need to consider this and decide if they are willing to set a goal for themselves that won't feel right initially and will take work to accomplish.

It is a lot easier for someone who is new to the game and has not established any bad habits. The first goal is to get the right grip, posture, and basic movement. A beginner's goal might be to learn enough so they feel confident to play on a course rather than a driving range. Or they may just need to learn how to make solid contact with the ball as opposed to the ground or, worse, whiffing altogether. When teaching beginners, it is important to look for progress and point out that progress to the new golfer so that they become ready to set the next goal.

I have made observable progress with many students, beginners all the way through to very low handicappers, in the very first lesson. Still, as with anything in life that's worth doing it takes time, practice, and patience. It doesn't all happen in just one lesson.

CHAPTER 2

FITTING YOUR GRIP

Developing My Method

"Good golf begins with a good grip."
  -Ben Hogan

I was recently awarded the PGA's specialized Teaching and Coaching certification. During the process I learned a lot that I have been able to incorporate into my teaching method. I found volumes of information on how to correct and encourage students. The importance of being aware of physical limitations was clearly pointed out in the coursework. I discovered that there are different theories about how people learn and that everyone learns differently even as it applies to sports. One such theory is Reissman's "styles of learning." In Reissman's view learners fall into three categories: visual learners, aural—those who learn by listening and performance learners. Another example is the theory put forth by Silver, Strong, and Perinini defining learning styles as "Mastery" (concrete, step-by-step practicality), "Understanding" (learning by reasoning and asking questions), "Self-expressive" (using feelings and emotions), and "Interpersonal" (one who only learns through social engagement and helping others).

This coursework gave me an appreciation of how differently people learn and how differently individuals' bodies affect their performance. This is how I became interested in the field of biomechanics as it applies to golf. I believe that when teaching is derived from biomechanics the swing will be more natural and fit the golfer's body, resulting in a better swing and better performance.

The field of biomechanics as it applies to the golf swing is fascinating. I soon noticed that players were coming to me with problem swings that they were having difficulty correcting. Sometimes they were even at the point of considering giving up golf altogether. I never want to see any student being discouraged to the point of leaving the game. I realized that most golf instruction uses the perfect swing model and since this is not fitted precisely to each individual this method forces the player to try to manipulate their swing, making improvement and accuracy complicated and difficult.

Trying to replicate a professional's perfect swing can be impossible for most average golfers due to their skill level and the difference in body types. Since they are not working with their body, they are working against it, and this will lead to more injuries, especially lower back, elbow, and wrist injuries.

To help the average golfer to progress and enjoy the game more I began to look for simple solutions from the field of biomechanics. I signed up for Mike Adams's PGA seminar on pressure plates, which was largely based in biomechanical theory. The seminar showed the importance of applying the correct pressure on the feet at exactly the correct time during the swing and synchronizing balance with the movement of the body. I gained a lot of useful information at Mike Adams's seminar, however, much of the teaching technique he introduced was based on sophisticated equipment and software not readily available to all golf instructors.

It seemed there should be a simpler method of helping to improve students' games that did not involve sophisticated equipment. I began researching and experimenting and I developed what I believe is a unique way to set up an individualized grip for each golf student that fits their body and is biomechanically correct for them.

To find a swing that fits one's unique anatomy and characteristics, to make them feel comfortable, and also eliminate the possibility of injuries, I start with finding a grip that would not require any manipulation of the club. This differentiates my method from many instructors who try to change the path of the ball flight by teaching students to hit from inside out or "flip." Often it is recommended that the player change their grip for different clubs. I recommend using the same grip for every club. Because once I have established a grip that works with the player's anatomy it will feel more comfortable—sometimes right away and sometimes with time. By using one grip for all clubs, players can get used to the grip and ensure that they will hit on the same plane every time without manipulation because the swing remains the same regardless of the club.

This seemingly small detail is the cornerstone of my teaching method. While the way you grip the club doesn't seem all that important, it actually plays a critical role in the biomechanics of your golf swing. It is also one of the simplest things to change and maintain consistently throughout the swing. The proper grip allows for a simpler and more natural-feeling swing that works with your body, not against it.

The idea behind my teaching method is not trying to copy the grip that tour players or professionals use, but to create your own grip. What is considered the "perfect golf grip" does not work for everyone. In fact, it works for very few. The grip that will work is the one that is set up specially for the individual golfer's body. The reason is obvious, everyone is built differently. For instance, the proportional length of the upper arm to the forearm is different from one player to the next, as is the full length of the arm and the proportion of the arm to the upper body and the torso. Further, posture is surprisingly a factor in setting up the proper grip. All these things pertaining to body size and shape coupled with posture change the way you should be griping the club, and your grip in turn will affect the plane of your swing.

Finding the Grip that Is Right for You

The following steps will outline how to find your "perfect grip." If you want to share this information with a friend, don't try to have them copy your grip. Instead, walk them through the following steps so they can find their own perfect grip. No doubt, it will be somewhat different from yours.

Step 1

I ask my students to stand straight with their legs together and allow their arms to hang naturally. The position of the hands, whether they turn in or hang straight, is dependent on the individual's posture.

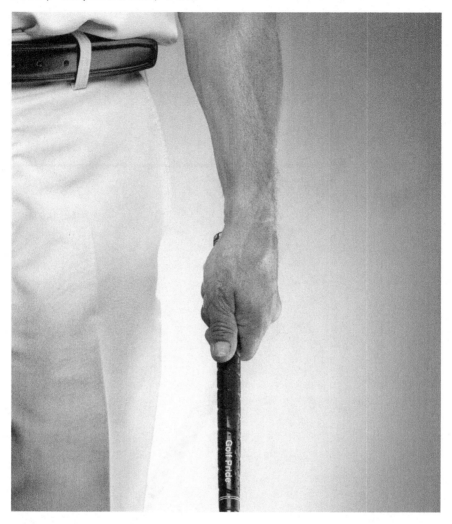

Don't change the natural position of your hand. Using the left hand (for a right-handed golfer) place the grip of the club in your hand lightly with the face of the club pointing toward the target. Now your left hand is in the correct position. Do not be tempted to change the position of the left hand as you follow the next steps to set up your grip.

Step 2

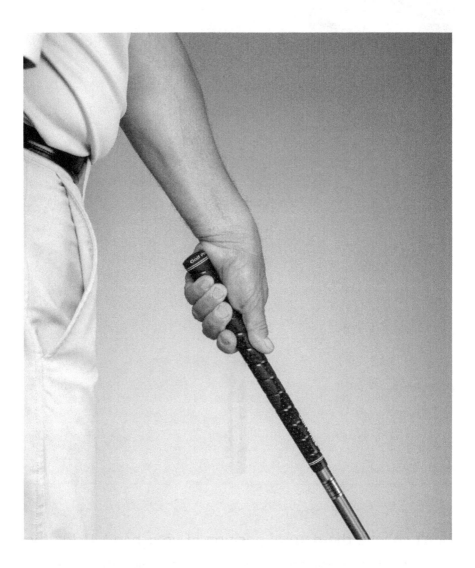

Keeping your left hand in the position established in Step 1, extend your left arm forward keeping the club head on the ground as far as you can comfortably reach forward without moving your upper body.

Step 3

Next, move the left foot to the side, parallel to the target line. For a person of average height, step out approximately 12 to 14 inches. You should be comfortable in this position and feel balanced. After stepping to the side, your left foot should be slightly open toward the target and the end of the grip should be pointing toward your navel. In this position, your left arm will be against your chest. Now you can feel a firm connection between your left arm and your chest.

Step 4

Then, without any movement in the left wrist, and keeping the arm to chest connection, bring the club to a 45-degree angle to the ground, i.e., to the after-impact body position. It is important to make sure that your balance is on the left foot and the right knee is bent toward the target. Your right heel is off the ground, as seen below. You will notice that in this position the face of the club points to the left of the target. Taking a swing and coming through with the club in this position will cause a hook and therefore require manipulation during the swing to correct it. This correction is not easily accomplished, and most golfers will be unsuccessful at making it on the fly.

Step 5

Instead, I ask my students to keep their wrist and their arm completely straight and turn their left forearm slightly so that the face of the club points exactly toward the target. All this is accomplished while holding the club only with the left hand. Left-handed players should do the exact opposite. When you correct the face of your club in this way, you correct your grip. In doing so you eliminate the source of many errors before you even start your swing. And you will have a lot less to think about as you initiate and follow through. Simpler is always better.

Step 6

After rotating your forearm slightly to the right so that the club face points directly toward the target, you should notice that your right arm is hanging freely slightly in front of your right leg. Now swing your right arm directly to meet the grip, keeping both arms completely straight and without any manipulation. With fully extended arms this creates the perfect hand position for your grip.

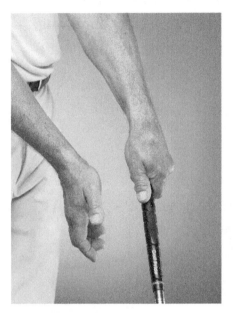 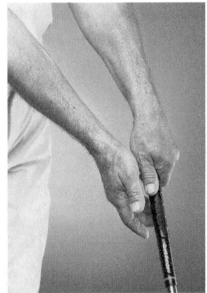

Step 7

Finally, you can return the head of the club to the right side of the ball or the starting position. Keep the grip you have just created for yourself intact. This is your perfect grip. Every now and then repeat this process to make sure that you haven't unconsciously changed something. Or maybe your posture has changed slightly, which would affect your grip. But generally speaking, this is the method and the grip you should keep for life.

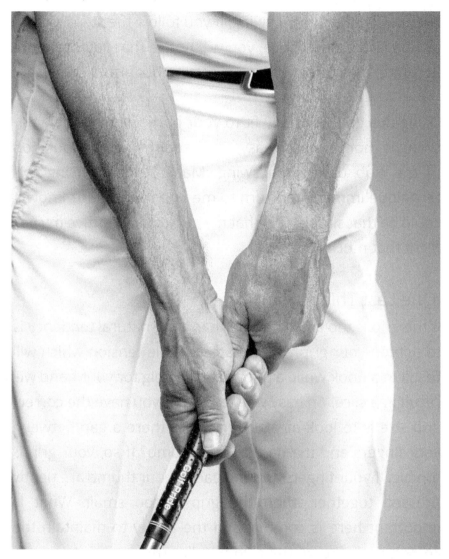

Your Perfect Grip

You will maintain this grip throughout the swing. There is no need to change it for different clubs either. Most golfers see immediate and dramatic results by setting up their grip using this method. You won't feel any restriction in your swing or the need to twist or manipulate the club in anyway.

Even with your current swing, if you follow the steps exactly as I have outlined above, you will notice that you are more accurate, improving not only direction but also distance.

Using this grip, uniquely fit to your body, you will feel your swing is more natural, easy, and requires no manipulation of the club during the swing. Many students using this technique immediately turn to me and say, "I didn't know it could be that simple!" or "that my grip could improve my ball flight that much!"

One Last Thing...Hand Size

If the grip is too small for your hand the natural tendency is to tighten your grip. This creates muscle tension which will result in a hook while a grip that is too big for your hand will result in a slice. An easy way to know if you have the correct grip size is to look at your fingers. Is there a gap between your fingers and the pad of your thumb? If so, your grip is too big. If your fingers and the pad of your thumb are tightly pressed together, then the grip is too small. What is important here is comfort and the ability to maintain the correct pressure on the club handle. The same is true with the positioning of your hand vertically. Notice that I grip the club close to the end. Some prefer a half inch or so sticking out above their hand. Again, in my view this is just a matter of preference.

CHAPTER 3

SETUP AND START RIGHT

From Beginner to PGA Professional

"Golf is a compromise between what your ego wants you to do, what experience tells you to do, and what your nerves let you do."

-Bruce Crampton

When I first came to the United States, I had to do whatever I could to make a living. One of those jobs was construction. One day, I happened to be working on a friend's house. I arrived early, ready to get started. He surprised me by saying, "Let's take the day off and play some golf." My first thought was, what is golf? Remember that golf was illegal in Communist Poland, so I had never heard of the game. In addition, I doubted my English, which was still not great. As students in Poland, we were all forced to study Russian. Today it is the opposite. Nearly all young people study and learn English in Poland by choice.

But once this friend explained what golf was to me, I had some idea. I had seen golf on TV once or twice here in the

States. Still, I knew nothing about how to play and had no equipment. Not letting this realty dissuade him, my friend gave me an old set of his clubs and tried to quickly give me some idea of how to swing a golf club. After about five minutes of instruction, I played my first nine holes of golf in Orange, Connecticut, at the Orange Hills Country Club. The starter put my friend and I together with two older gentlemen who played short but quite straight, with the experience of age and years of playing. I was happy and somewhat amazed that my tee shot was longer than everyone else's. My second shot was ok, I ended up near the green but then, of course, I didn't know how to chip. I sculled the ball and took two shots to finish with a bogey. My friend hit to the right, into the rough, and finished with a bogey as well. Pretty good for a first hole, I thought. But my friend put it down to beginner's luck.

The next hole was a par 5. I finished this hole as a double par, i.e., a 10. I was quickly figuring out that I had a lot to learn and that's when my journey began. When you don't know how to play, every golf course seems to be full of trees, bunkers, and way too much water. You begin to realize how long the journey will be. How patient you will need to be and how much sweat you will have to invest.

Even so, from the first time I played I knew I loved the game. I decided then and there that I wanted to improve. I knew it was a game that I could enjoy for the rest of my life. I invested in a set of clubs. Kmart offered a set of cast iron clubs for a little over $100. This was years ago. It seemed like a lot of money at the time. But I was hooked.

I couldn't afford to play on golf courses regularly, so I went to the driving range and after some practice I decided to try playing on a golf course for the second time. I broke three of the clubs that same day. Not in the way you might think, by getting angry and throwing them. No, they broke accidently. The heads broke on three of the clubs without even hitting the ground just by contacting the ball because they were cast iron and so cheaply made. It took me awhile to save enough to buy my second set of clubs. But at least these clubs lasted a bit longer. I bought them in a golf shop. They had been a demo set but they served the purpose.

Learning to play golf was a challenge but I've always enjoyed challenging myself. I tried to get on a golf course once a month, usually midday Saturday when the weekend rates were the lowest. I went to the golf range in Milford, Connecticut, which has since gone out of business. Often, I went just to watch other golfers and see how they hit. What did they have in common? What were they doing that I would want to avoid? I learned a lot about what to do and what not to do this way. I also frequented Barnes and Noble looking for books, always books on golfing. I looked for examples of the best players in the history of golf. That's how I first discovered Ben Hogan and his book The Five Lessons, as well as Power Golf. In addition to Ben Hogan, I became acquainted with Bobby Jones and Sam Snead.

Ben Hogan stood out for me. I was aware that many people thought he was the best golfer in history. I started researching Hogan more than any of the other players. There was something special about him. I respected the way he came back from a car accident that nearly killed him and relearned golf. He didn't let anything stop him. I noticed the fluidity of his swing. I thought that if I wanted to learn the game, I needed to study and analyze the best swings and try to find aspects of them I could emulate.

Bobby Jones was an amateur golfer. What impressed me most about him was his passion for the game and how that led him to compete and win against professionals. I found out that he was a person who loved to give advice. He wanted to give back to the game so that others could improve and become world-class golfers like he was. Reading about Bobby and studying his technique I was struck by the importance of body rotation. And not just rotation but staying centered during the rotation. I began watching his series How I Play Golf. I learned a great deal about his technique in different parts of the game, e.g., driving, bunker play, and putting. I enjoyed watching the movie about him, The Grand Slam.

What I learned from Sam Snead was the importance of tempo. I noted the way he recentered his body and his lateral movement in the beginning of the downswing. But what really impressed me about Sam Snead was how much fun he had with the game. The average player often gets angry and disappointed, and many times at the end of eighteen holes they are ready to quit. Not Sam, anytime you watched him play you could see how much joy he took from it. I looked up to Sam because I planned to improve and to play well but I wanted to enjoy myself at the same time and not take it too seriously. I wanted to learn to control my body and my mind, not to let the game control me.

When Sam Snead was playing golf in the 1950s and 1960s with Ben Hogan and Byron Nelson, they were the top players of their time. I was still a child in Poland in the 1960s, not around yet for most of the 1950s. But when I started to get truly interested in golf here in the US, I began searching YouTube to see what I could learn from these greats. I especially looked for slow motion videos of their swings. At night after work, I would play and replay these images of golf history, poring over them. I couldn't help feeling lucky to have this luxury especially when I recalled the small black-and-white TV with its grainy reception and limited programming that I had to fight over with my brothers to watch.

Since I did not take up golf as a very young person, I needed to invest more time into studying golf. All that analysis and study helped me to create my own path and teaching method.

Setup

The first thing about your setup is to make sure you have your feet in the correct position. For most shots your feet should be separated, just slightly outside of the width of your shoulders. If you are using a driver, use a slightly wider stance. For wedges, your feet should be a bit closer together. For instance, just two inches shy of the width of your shoulders.

For right-handed golfers the right foot should be perpendicular (or at 90 degrees) to the target line. The left foot is slightly open, this is to say your toes should be pointing at about 25 to 30 degrees toward the target. Your heels remain the same distance apart as described above. This puts you into a toed-out or half duck-footed stance. In other words, one foot is pointing straight in front of you while the other, the leading foot (or left foot for a right-handed player) is toed out.

The position of the ball is also very important. There are two dimensions to take into consideration. First, where to place the ball horizontally or left to right. Simply stated, the ball position for all irons should be about one inch left of the center of your stance. In other words, one inch closer to the leading foot (to the left for right-handed players, to the right for left-handed players).

The driver is different. With the driver, you are hitting from a tee and thus catching the ball on the upswing. In this case for the average golfer, the tee is placed in front of an imaginary line draw forward from your left heel.

The second dimension is where to place the ball in front of you or how far you should stand away from the ball. The best way to find the correct distance to the ball is to stand in an upright position with both hands on the club. Taking a proper grip, which is explained in Chapter 2, hold the club parallel to the ground. For men, the upper arms should be resting on the front of the chest, for women, slightly on the sides of the chest. See the following picture.

Next release your wrists so that the club hangs freely downward. Be sure to maintain a firm grip only relaxing your wrists. The wrist position will be similar to the wrist position at the moment of impact.

From this position with straight knees, bend your upper body from the waist until the club touches the ground. Now, bend your knees slightly, just so they are not locked.

From where your club landed, the ball should be placed toward the toe or the front of the club, even though your goal is to contact the ball in the center. This is because during the swing, centrifugal force will tend to stretch the joints in your arms and wrists. As a result, if you were to place the ball exactly in the center of the club head, you would naturally be pulled somewhat forward and contact the ball at the heel of the club. This can cause something that no golfer wants to see, a shank. A shank is caused by hitting the ball close to the shaft, near the heel which sends the ball sharply to the right.

Another way of finding the distance to the ball is to make a quarter swing with your body leaning forward. While doing this, keep your left arm completely straight and tight to your body. Note where the club head touches the ground. Be sure not to use your hands as you swing and not to manipulate your swing in any way. Let the swing flow naturally. If the club is not touching the ground during this exercise your body position is too upright. On the other hand, if the club hits the ground too early (behind the ball), this indicates that you are leaning too far forward.

CHAPTER 4

HOMEWORK & CORRECTIONS

Scarcity and Change

"Mistakes are part of the game. It's how well you recover from them, that's the mark of a great player."
  – Alice Cooper

Growing up money was very tight. I understood that you had to work hard just to survive. My mother's way of encouraging me to study and get an education was to say, "Don't expect me to reward you for getting good grades. You are doing that for yourself, so that you won't have to sweep streets later." Everyone who was capable of working had to work, including children. So, at a very young age I started working and giving my earnings to my parents. In communist Poland, you never knew exactly how much you made. The government would take as much out in taxes as it wanted, and you got what was left in your paycheck.

Notwithstanding my mother's dire warnings, homework was not at the top of my priority list. I did what I had to get by. But what I really enjoyed was trying new activities. As a teenager I tried everything I could: volleyball, ice hockey, life guarding, motor racing, and even acting in local theater. Later, as I worked to become specialized in teaching and coaching golf, I learned that exposure to a variety of different sports as a youth is the best way to develop natural talent and excel in the sport of your choice later in life.

When I was in elementary school in Poland, there were not many organized team sports with the financial backing to provide the necessary equipment to play the game, never mind safety equipment. We often had to supply our own equipment in school for the games we played in physical education.

My friends and I would organize games after school and on weekends. Mostly we played in the streets, in our backyards, or even in the WWII cemetery next to my home. Often, we improvised our own equipment. We even built our own hockey rink by shoveling the snow in the backyard, packing it, and then hosing it down with water.

After elementary school we had to take a high school placement test and we were assigned to an educational track based on our test results. I was sent to one of the best high schools for college-bound students. It was called a technical school but that does not have the same connotation as it does in English. This school specialized in the areas of math and science. I had wanted to study medicine and become a doctor, but the state decided I would become a computer technician.

One day I heard that there would be trials for the National Junior Ice Hockey League. It would be an opportunity to skate on groomed ice in a real stadium and be coached. I was fifteen years old. I qualified for the first of two Junior levels. I played left-wing offense. After a few months of training twice a week for two to three hours a day, the league found it did not have enough money to continue, and to my disappointment it folded.

I continued to participate in sports throughout high school, joining the swim team, track and field, and handball teams. In the winter, I took up volleyball. My team decided to practice after school, so we contacted the women's team from the medical school near us who played volleyball on the National Level. They agreed to practice with us. In the beginning they were beating us 15–0 or 15–1 if we were lucky. Gradually we began to give them some competition. Because of what we learned from this practice, our school placed second in the state school championship. I was invited to play on the third national level for one season, but again the money ran out and the team was disbanded.

Speedway motor racing was very popular in Poland. I had gone to watch races with my father and brothers since I was quite young. When I got my driver's license at fifteen, I hoped to drive in the speedway, so I secretly went for my motorcycle license. A friend of mine who was just a couple years older than me had been competing for two years. Unfortunately, he was involved in a serious accident. He suffered a traumatic brain injury. This unhappy event was more than enough to keep my parents from signing the necessary permission forms for me to compete. Looking back, it was for the best.

Through it all I was lucky enough to take advantage of more opportunities than many of my friends. I learned that nothing good in life comes without hard work and practice. And while I was not introduced to golf, the sport that I love, until later in life, I had laid the groundwork to learn.

Corrections

When I make any correction or change to a student's swing, I always explain how the correction will help them improve their game. I like them to understand why they are making the necessary change. Understanding why they are asked to do something a certain way can help to avoid hesitancy in making the change and/or backsliding into old habits. During your own lessons, you may find it beneficial to ask why, to find out how a recommended adjustment will improve your game.

Oddly enough as I explain the way I want my students to swing, they will frequently say "That's what I'm doing now!" Sometimes people are unaware of how they are actually performing. I like to video my students so they can see exactly what they are doing. Often, they are surprised because the video helps them to see what I see. This simple step of showing someone what they are doing can be enough to achieve the desired results and usually it does work. I recommend that you set up a tripod and video yourself. You may be surprised at what you see.

But sometimes even this does not help. During one lesson, I videoed a student. He could see what he was doing wrong based on my explanation and I showed him how to correct his swing. But he told me it wasn't comfortable. The correct movement, stance, or grip may not feel comfortable at first but how comfortable is it to continue making bad shots and trying to recover from them? It is a choice that must be made to see real improvement. Some people would rather not improve than feel uncomfortable, or they fool themselves into thinking they can do it another way.

Often when I watch a tournament on TV, I hear the commentator analyzing a swing using the phrase "on the downswing you have to clear your left hip." This is definitively not the case. Clearing your hip will destroy the balance between your upper and lower body and result in either a hook or a slice.

The changes I usually recommend are not huge changes, but they will often make a big difference. Even so, I find that most students cannot make more than two corrections to their swing at a time or during one lesson. I try not to overload a lesson and give the student too much to think about.

Practice Between Lessons

So, I will only give my students one or two adjustments to keep in mind. I ask them to concentrate on one thing at a time. First, practice on the driving range. When they feel pretty comfortable on the driving range, I ask them to try their new skills on the golf course where conditions will be more variable and there will be distractions. I ask that they practice as often as possible and consider one lesson every week or every other week. This usually gives them enough time to implement the changes I suggest.

The Clubs - Having the Right Tools

Are clubs and club fitting important? In my opinion, the answer is yes and no. So here is the point, if you are an adult who is just starting out, it is not so important to have an amazing set of clubs fitted exactly for you. As you learn and develop, your swing will change, and you will need to be fitted again. All that money will be wasted. When starting out, I recommend that you have clubs that are the correct length and shaft flex for you. Shaft flex is the amount a club will bend during the swing. The correct shaft flex depends on the speed of your swing. The faster your swing, the more the club will flex. So, if you are starting with a fast swing, you will need a stiffer shaft. The slower the swing, the more flexible the shaft should be. Even if you are going to buy used clubs, you should talk to a pro or go to any golf shop and they will be able to advise you. But at this point it's probably not worth overspending. There will be plenty of time for that as you develop your game!

It is a different story for young players. There is a tendency for parents to want to start their child on a hand-me-down set or to cut the shaft to make it shorter. Children have not yet developed the strength in their bodies or their bones for this type of club. Cut-down clubs are way too heavy for a child and when they try to compensate, they will develop bad habits. A child will also be more susceptible to injury in this case, for instance a strained wrist or spine. An early sports injury can last a lifetime. To help prevent injury and get off to the right start it is important to buy a good set of clubs designed for young players. Make sure that the clubs are the correct length and weight for the child's size and physical ability. A "youth player" is a child from around three to sixteen years of age. By sixteen most children can begin to use a somewhat heavier club. Of course, it is still dependent on the individual's development, the size and strength of the child, as to whether they are ready to move on to a heavier adult club.

As an adult player develops and their swing is more established and consistent, the correct clubs and club fitting become much more important. As you may remember, I previously mentioned my second set of clubs. They were Yonex. My golfing friends laughed at me because they said when I swung the club it looked like I was fishing. I didn't know any better at the time, but I was sold senior clubs that were so flexible I had to slow down my swing so that I would be able to hit straight. I still had to play with these clubs for a few years before I felt I could afford another set. Once I had a chance to buy a new set it was a difficult transition to the stiffer clubs. I had become accustomed to compensating. This demonstrates why it is so important once you have some control over your game to be fitted properly.

What is most important about the clubs you choose? What should you be looking for? The length needs to fit you. If they are too long, the heel of the club will hit the ground and most likely your ball will fly left. If they are too short, you will tend to hit the ball with the toe of the club head, then everything you hit will go right. In addition to length, the flex must be correct for the speed of your swing, the faster the swing the stiffer the club needs to be and the slower the swing the reverse is true.

Clubs are produced using a variety of different materials. The best clubs are made of forged material, not cast iron. Club shafts are either made of steel or graphite. Steel shafts are a little heavier. Some people like this kind of feeling. Graphite shafts are lighter than steel. Some people believe that because graphite is lighter it is only for older players. This is not true. You can get a stiff shaft on a graphite club, in which case it can be very suitable for a younger player or a player with a strong, fast swing. It's all about the feel and personal preference. Today shafts are also made in a combination of steel and graphite. This, again, is a matter of feel and personal preference.

There can be a temptation to use the same clubs played by your favorite professional. I knew of a golfer who admired Tiger Woods. He requested that his clubs be built exactly like the clubs that Tiger Woods plays with, assuming that this would help improve his game. He spent around $300 per club and once he began using these clubs his game fell apart completely. Nothing was going right for him. The feel of the clubs was all wrong for him. He finally came to realize that not having the same body or ability as Tiger he could not play with the same clubs. Don't buy clubs because your favorite PGA tour player is using them. Buy the clubs that fit you best.

When you are at a point in your game that makes sense for you to invest in a great set of clubs, talk to a professional who can assess your swing correctly. Ask for a full club fitting. Make sure they try your swing using different brands, weights, and materials. They will also be able to recommend the correct length and flex for you. When your clubs are right for you, the difference is instantaneous. You will immediately hit farther and more accurately. When you hit multiple balls on the range, you will notice the dispersion of ball landings will be significantly smaller and it is possible to increase your yardage between ten and twenty yards for each club.

CHAPTER 5

PUTTING

Go/No Go Career Decisions

"In any moment of decision, the best thing you can do is the right thing, the next best thing is the wrong thing, and the worst thing you can do is nothing."
  -Theodore Roosevelt

Putting is all about making good choices. We make choices all the time, but it can be difficult to know at the moment we are making the decision if it is the right one. Will this decision make things better or worse, lead to success or failure? One of the biggest decisions and risks of my life was to change careers midlife and pursue a PGA certification.

For one thing, it was hardly my first career change. At eighteen I was forced into military service in Poland and rose to the rank of Corporal in charge of about three hundred troops. In school I was trained to be a computer technician. Since jobs were hard to come by in Poland and especially jobs that paid well, I was, for a brief time, a taxi driver. This allowed me to save enough money for my flight to the United States. Believe it or not, this was a highly sought after position and required not only a driving test but also a written exam that proved I had memorized the names and locations of the approximately 1,200 streets in the city of Torun.

After eighteen months of driving all day and into the night, for as long as I could stay awake, I earned enough to secure my ticket to the United States on a Russian-built airplane. This plane was considerably smaller than today's planes. My knees were practically pushed into my chest. The guy sitting next to me on the aisle went to sleep immediately and I couldn't budge him for the entire nine-hour flight. But somehow, I made it to the US with five dollars in my pocket and the hope that my uncle would remember to pick me up at the airport.

I've mentioned earlier that when I came to the United States, I did not speak English. In order to survive, I began washing dishes, a job that required very little knowledge of the English language and even less training.

Of course, I had plans to better myself. I wanted to be part of the society I was living in. I had dreams of becoming an American citizen and improving my career prospects as well. I was determined to learn English. I attended adult education classes at the local high school.

When I wasn't working or taking classes, I usually had the TV on, trying to learn the meaning of the words by watching the action. I remember the first English word I picked up was "because." It sounded familiar to me since one of my favorite Polish dishes is pronounced similarly. Bigos is a hearty stew that is made with mushrooms, smoked and cured meat, and sauerkraut. And that is how I started learning English, through association.

Subsequently, I worked construction, I delivered newspapers, took jobs in pretty much anything I could find. Finally, by learning English and with no small amount of luck I landed a job in a machine factory. Eventually, I was promoted to department manager. The pay was quite good, especially considering the income-earning potential I left behind in Poland, but it was far from my dream job. It involved long hours in confined spaces, and repetitive tasks. The more I thought about it the more I imagined a life that centered around golf

I took the leap. I quit my job and started a company building, fitting, and repairing golf clubs. I called my company Golf Smarter because the spineing technique I used improved the direction of the club head and thus helped create a straighter shot. It wasn't too much of a stretch for me to build and repair clubs given my experience in machining at the factory. But selling my services was an uphill battle. I spent my days going from golf club to golf club, to sporting goods stores and repair shops, asking if they needed help with club repair.

Most places already had someone who handled repairs. I had some limited success. I had built a website but, there again, traffic had to be pushed toward the site and competition was stiff. It was clear that I would need to bring in a lot more work if I was going to support myself and help my family. Then one day I walked into the Connecticut Golf Club and lightning struck. They needed full-time help in the cart barn and I took the job. Not only was I lucky enough to find work that would give me health benefits and a steady, albeit low income, I also found a club that was willing to help me become a PGA Professional. It was a long and difficult road, but the rest is history.

Putting

The choices you need to make in putting mainly center around three areas: distance control, direction control, and reading the green. Distance control can be summed up simply. It is how hard you hit the ball or the amount of force you put behind it that will determine the distance, all other things being equal. Directional control is a matter of choosing the line toward which you want to hit the ball. Finally, reading the green is an art but there is some science involved. Directional control and reading the green are closely tied together.

Distance Control Distance control is the most important and happily the easiest to achieve if you have the right approach. But of course, it still takes work and focus. Distance control is more important than directional control because if you hit one foot to the left or to the right you can still make the putt. But statistically speaking if you hit the ball ten feet too far you will have much more trouble making it to the hole.

Directional control becomes more important the shorter the distance to the hole. The closer you are to the hole, within the last four or five feet, things begin to change, and now direction becomes more important than distance control.

For example, when you hit the ball hard enough to make a distance of twenty feet, there is enough energy to carry the ball on its way. Alternatively, when you hit softly for a shorter putt, there is less energy holding the ball on route so, the slope and gravity will start to take the ball in different directions. With longer putts the energy you need to put into your swing tends to carry the ball in the desired direction. As you get closer to the hole, the necessary light tap does not provide enough energy to keep the ball on its trajectory past irregularities in the green and the ball path becomes very susceptible to variations in the shape of the green.

There are two primary methods of distance control, one is referred to as "feel" and the other is "mechanical." The first method is just what it sounds like. You feel or intuit the distance you need to hit the ball. The mechanical approach is about measuring how many steps away from the hole you are and/or how far back you need to move your putter in order to make the distance.

In general, most people tend to identify as being "feelers" or instinctual putters. In my experience most golfers like to think that they are feelers. My guess is that people think it seems to demonstrate a more innate, natural talent. However, the reality is very different. Most people are actually mechanical putters.

Knowing that someone is a mechanical putter actually makes it a lot easier to work on distance control. I watch my students try to make three putts each from a different direction and different length. A feeler will come close (within at least two feet of the hole) or sink the putt each time. If not, I know they are mechanical putters.

The way to develop a mechanical style of putting is first to measure in walking steps, not by feet. This automatically makes it easier to measure the distance. Then, put three balls in a line and hit a comfortable easy swing toward the center of the green in a flat area. Just hit, do not pay attention between putts as to how far the ball is going.

These three balls will usually travel about the same distance. Now count the walking steps the ball has traveled. For instance, each of the three balls may have gone an average of nine steps from where the putt initiated. If this is true, you know that using about half the intensity of your comfortable swing will send the ball approximately four and a half steps. Conversely, twice the intensity will send your putt about eighteen steps. If you have an uphill lie add a couple "steps" to your calculation of swing intensity. For a downhill lie, deduct steps.

Reading the Green

It is difficult, if not impossible, to separate directional control from reading the green, and reading the green will be your biggest challenge. First you need to find the fall line. If you imagine pouring a bucket of water on the green and visualize where the water would run, that is the fall line. And that is the direction in which the ball will roll.

On a flat green, the fall line is the straightest and shortest path to the hole. There are many ways to figure out the fall line. Each golfer seems to have his or her own personal preference. I look at the cup. I stand approximately five feet away from the hole. Then I look at the shape of the cup behind the pin. If the pin appears to be dead center and the size and shape of the cup on either side of the pin look equal, you are on the fall line. If they are not, you are not on the fall line. You need to step to the side and reorient yourself until you find it. The diagram below illustrates what I mean.

On the fall line   Off the fall line

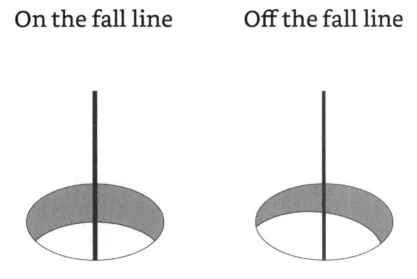

Once I know where the fall line is, I mentally draw a circle around the hole with the distance between the lie of the ball and the hole, defining the radius of the circle. Then I divide the imaginary circle into quadrants.

To read the green correctly, you need to define the quadrant that your ball is in. Then think of dividing that quadrant in half to form the eighth of the circle where your ball lies. Look at the diagram on the following page, the quadrants and sections are numbered.

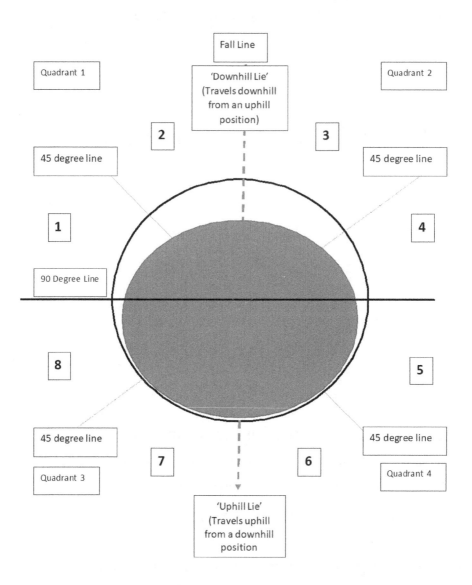

When the hole is lower than the ball, it is referred to as a "downhill lie" because you will need to hit the ball in the downhill direction or the direction of the fall line. Conversely, when the hole is higher than the ball, it is referred to as an "uphill lie."

If your ball is in section 1, it is referred to as a side lie. From this position you want to cross the 45-degree line, into section 2, without crossing the fall line. Once the ball crosses the fall line you will miss the cup. A similar action is required on the opposite side in section 4, which is also a side lie. From section 4 the ball needs to enter the hole through section 3. Sections 5 and 8 are considered side lies as well, and because you are hitting uphill the putt is by definition heading in the opposite direction as the fall line. If you hit toward the center of the cup, the ball will end up short and roll back to you in the direction of the fall line.

Think of it like a free throw in basketball. The ball cannot be thrown straight into the basket. The ball has to go above the basket and then fall back down into the basket as it loses energy. So, from section 8 you need to cross the 90-degree line and enter near or above the 45-degree line between sections 1 and 2. The longer the putt, the farther into section 2 you will need to send the ball in order to make the putt. Section 5 is the mirror image of section 8. From section 5 you need to aim toward the 45-degree line between sections 3 and 4.

When you are in sections 2, 3, 6, and 7 you simply aim toward the fall line. The only difference is that from sections 6 and 7 you will be hitting uphill from an uphill lie, therefore you will need to put somewhat more energy into the swing action verses the energy used for a downhill lie (sections 2 and 3).

In addition to the items mentioned above, you should be aware of the speed of the greens. The best way to find out how fast the greens are is to try them. On a fast green, as the name implies, your ball will roll more easily. While each golf course you play may have a different green speed, the greens on any one golf course should all be the same speed. Generally, you can trust the green speed to remain the same from hole to hole on most private golf courses. On public courses, you will want to be more careful, as the speeds may tend to vary.

Posture

As far as posture goes, this is personal preference. It does not matter how upright your posture is or how much you bend over. Use the same grip and posture as always. The old-school approach to putting maintains that your eye should be above the ball. Practically speaking, this does not work and usually causes a miss that curves to the left of the hole. Eye position depends on how close you are to the ball. If you stand too close, it doesn't matter where your eye is vis-à-vis the ball.

It is important to stand at the distance from the ball where your club swings in a straight line toward where you want to hit. This means that as you swing, the line drawn by the head of your club does not form an arc. If you are too close to the ball, the head of your putter will arc outside the line. If you are too far away, it will arc inside to inside. If you are too far, move closer to the ball and slide your grip down until the putter swings straight on the intended line without changing your posture. Once you find the correct hand position on the grip of your putter you can mark that spot because, keeping your posture constant, your grip should always be in the same place. Adjust your distance to the ball accordingly.

Two Types of Putting Strokes

There are two different types of putting strokes. One is a pendulum motion, in which the putter moves the same amount on the backswing as it does on the follow through. Be careful not to bend your leading wrist or rush your swing. These are common mistakes. The danger with the pendulum approach is that if your backswing is too long the tendency will be to decelerate, making it more difficult to control the distance. The second method is controlled acceleration. With this method, make the backswing one measure and the follow through two measures, or twice as long. The longer forward motion guarantees acceleration and, thus, more control. If, for example, the backstroke is ten inches, you must pass the ball by twenty inches.

CHAPTER 6

CHIPPING

Exotic Golf Courses

"A leading difficulty with the average player is that he totally misunderstands what is meant by concentration. He may think he is concentrating hard when he is merely worrying."
-Bobby Jones

As a rule, I do not play golf on my time off. This is one of the ways I try to keep my relationship with my wife on a good footing. I feel that vacation time is our time together and, to be fair, I have plenty of time to play golf during the season at the Connecticut Golf Club in Easton, Connecticut where I work and teach. However, when we travel somewhere exotic, where the golf courses are interesting and we may not have the opportunity to return soon, my wife often suggests or even coaxes me to play. That is exactly what happened in Jamaica in 2013.

I had the opportunity to play the White Witch, an amazing golf course designed by Robert von Hagge and Rick Baril. The course has an interesting history. It was at one time the Rose Hall Plantation, owned by a wealthy Briton named John

Palmer and his wife Annie. Legend has it that Annie still haunts the area the course is built on. The rumor is that Annie Palmer was orphaned, then learned witchcraft as a child from her adopted mother. She treated the plantation slaves poorly and killed three of her husbands in their sleep. Historians debate the veracity of this claim, but it lends a certain dark fascination to the area.

This course is startlingly beautiful. The holes are mostly elevated, so you can view the water from nearly every hole. The fairways are so soft it feels like walking on plush carpeting. One of the episodes on the golf channel's Big Break was filmed on the White Witch. You would assume that the course would be very popular. But on this particular day, my wife and I were the only people there, outside of the staff. We could not imagine why. Apparently, it was the first week that the course had reopened under new management and the fact that it was open was not yet widely known. We felt like we owned the golf course. The staff was so friendly and the bar cart followed us for eighteen holes since no one else was there. We had a cart and a caddy, but we did not see Annie while we were there.

The first hole is a par 5 going downhill to a narrow fairway. The second shot on this hole is very picturesque and interesting. It is a difficult uphill shot that doglegs right to an elevated green, which was intimidating, but turned out to be not as bad as it looked.

Then there was a par 3 that went downhill over a steep volcanic rock ravine. Below was a small pond at the bottom of the ravine. The green was not deep, but it was wide from right to left. The views were so magnificent it was almost difficult to concentrate on the game. The distance to the green looked like it was farther than the yardage that was showing. So, I used one club up against the caddie's recommendation and I hit over the green into the rough. The moral of the story is trust the caddie. He knows the distance.

The last hole goes uphill to the club house. We noticed two more cars in the parking lot and it seemed strange to suddenly see someone else at "our" golf club. I almost wished there were more than eighteen holes to play!

Recently, I was in Iceland looking for a golf course to play. Iceland was the exact opposite of Jamaica. Everything I saw was flat, rocky, and moonlike. I called a couple golf clubs looking to budget expenses and was quoted a fee for nine holes and for twelve holes. I could not understand why they would quote for twelve holes. I joked that maybe it was a nine-hole golf course and people liked to play an extra three holes. It made no sense. Finally, I realized that because of the limited area to build on, they had actually designed a twelve-hole golf course.

I played the El Camaleon Golf course in Cancun, Mexico, not even a month after the Mayakoba Classic tournament was played there. Since I happened to be staying close by, I wanted to experience this golf course. I had watched the tournament on TV. But there is a big difference between seeing a course on TV and playing the course yourself. Even so, I recognized some of the holes I had seen during the PGA tournament. The practice area was well designed with chipping, pitching, putting, and bunker areas. I remember I was assigned to play with a golfer from Indiana. He asked what tees I wanted to play from. I told him that I would like to experience playing from the black tees (the championship tees), to see what the tour players saw when they stood on the tee. He told me it was crazy to play that long. He chose to play from the white (men's) tees.

Four holes in particular were very memorable. The first hole was a par 5. In the entry to the fairway near the landing area, there was a large rock. When I got closer, I saw that it was not a rock but rather a cave. So, my ball could have rolled into the cave and been lost for good. I played to the right and got on the green. Today's tour players are hitting so far, they will typically hit past the rock.

As we played the second hole, a par 3, we encountered a long iguana right next to the tee. It must have been about five feet long and it would not move. We were unsure of how to deal with the situation until it finally moved of its own accord. Surprisingly, it was better to be shorter than to hit over the green here because past the green there was another cave and in that cave there was a snake pit. A bad place to try to retrieve a ball. Fortunately, I hit onto the green. On another challenging par 3, the rough slopes steeply toward the green on the left while on the right side there is a cliff that plunges twenty feet straight down to the water.

From the tee you could just make out the edge of the cliff, but you could not tell how steep the drop-off was. The twelfth hole was another par 3. It was right next to the ocean. The wind was so strong that I had to hit about 45 degrees toward the water and the wind took my ball back to the green. My ball landed on the green successfully, but the wind kept the ball rolling past the hole to the left side of the green.

I also had the opportunity to play the Kauai Lagoons Golf Club on the island of Kauai. It is the only course designed by Jack Nicklaus in Hawaii. The most memorable part of this course was driving over the hardened volcanic lava. Kauai Lagoons features the longest continuous stretch of oceanfront in all of Hawaii. It is quite stunning!

Another memorable golf outing was at the Olde Florida Country Club. I had been invited to play by a member of the club I work at in Connecticut. The member pointed to a rock in front of us. He asked if I saw it. He already knew what I found out when we came closer. It was a ten-foot alligator. The alligator was in what appeared to be his "favorite spot." He had been sitting near the hole guarding his territory on and off for a number of years. My host for the day asked me to go closer for a better picture. I opted not to do so. In tropical locations such as these it is not uncommon to find unwelcome guests.

Chipping

The simple definition of chipping is when the ball is in the air for less distance than the distance it rolls on the green. Chipping refers to the shot you make when the ball is just outside the green. If it is a large green, it can be a relatively long shot. If it is a smaller green, the shot could be as short as five to ten feet. When you are off the green, but close to it, you chip. This means that your shot should be low and it should roll. Because for most, it is easier to control the length of roll than to control the distance in the air.

It is similar to putting in that the closer the ball is to the hole, the shorter your backswing should be. If the ball is in the rough around the green or still on the fairway, but close to the green, you should chip. The goal is to place the ball as close to the hole as possible and finish with one putt. If you are in deep rough or have an uphill or downhill lie it's called a specialty shot. You can read about this in Chapter 9.

There are two different schools of thought when it comes to chipping. One is to use the same swing for different distances but use different clubs. For instance, when you use a 60-degree wedge the ball will go higher with more back spin due to the loft of the wedge. After the ball lands, it will stop a lot sooner than it would using a 9-iron, for example. This is because the 9-iron has a lower loft, so the trajectory of the ball will be lower and the ball will roll farther.

Think of watering a lawn with a hose. When you point the hose up high, the water tends to fall almost straight down and splash. When the hose is pointed lower the water will go farther, not splashing in all directions but rather pushing forward.

The second method of chipping is to use the same club for any distance and vary the length of the backswing. This second method is my method. I use the same club around the green, a 60-degree wedge on all shots that are eighty-five yards or less except, of course, when putting. This is because the length and the weight of the club remains constant for all these shots. In this way, you can get used to the feel and weight of the club. For longer distances the backswing is longer, with the opposite being true for shorter distances.

My setup for chipping starts with the face of the club pointing toward the target. The ball should be placed in the center of your stance. Now walk forward toward the ball. Then slide your grip down the club until the head of the club is flat on the ground. When the head is flat to the ground, take your normal grip. Without changing the direction of the club face, point the toes of both feet slightly to the left. Now your hips and shoulders will naturally be pointing a little to the left. But to be accurate you must change the angle of the shoulders. Leave your hips pointing to the left and turn your shoulders toward the target line (the intended path you want the ball to take). Keep your left arm very straight and your right elbow relaxed.

Now you are ready to chip by rocking your shoulders back and forth, similar to a regular putting stroke. The mistake to avoid here is allowing the wrists to move. Make sure that there is no movement in the wrists as you chip.

The club you choose to use for chipping will be based on personal preference. With practice you will find out how far and how high you can hit with a given club. With my 60-degree wedge, I find my ball is in the air about 40 percent of the distance and rolling about 60 percent of the distance on a flat green.

Each wedge is designed to have a "bounce" that keeps the club from going deep into the ground. The bounce refers to the angle between the ground and the leading edge of the club. If your swing is steep, you will tend to make a larger divot and need a higher degree of bounce, for example 12 or 14 degrees. If your swing is flat, your club will slide along the ground and you need a smaller bounce, maybe 6 or 8 degrees. Hitting the ground too hard can cause injuries. Using the correct bounce for your swing will prevent this from happening.

CHAPTER 7

PITCHING

Solidarity and Military Service

"The mind messes up more shots than the body."
– Tommy Bolt

For me, military service was not a choice. It was required, as it was for all young Polish men aged eighteen. I was called as soon as I finished school and was forced to serve. It was a time of upheaval in Poland called "Solidarity" and not a great time to be completing my obligatory service.

Solidarity began as a workers' movement in Communist Poland. In the 1970s the communist party had been cracking down on labor parties. Problems stemming from Poland's slow economy fueled discontent. Polish nationalism and pro-American sentiment were growing, and by the 1980s these forces came together to form what was referred to as the Solidarity Movement. The movement was supported by the Catholic Church and liberal anti-communists. Many people are not aware that the movement was also aided financially by the CIA. Our only information about world events was provided by Radio Free Europe, which was broadcast by the United States.

During this time, the Polish government was essentially fighting its own citizens, its workers who were asking for fair working conditions. In this sense, a civil war was raging in Poland. At the same time, everyone was afraid that the Soviet Union would take advantage of the situation and invade Poland from the outside.

As part of the military training I received in the Polish Army, I was warned that we might have to defend the government against our friends, neighbors, and even our family. We were told that if we refused to shoot them, "they" would not hesitate to shoot us from behind.

Happily, it never came to that and I was discharged from the army and made my way to America in 1988, one year before Lech Wałęsa was elected President of Poland in the first free election since 1947.

When I left Poland, the Solidarity Movement had just begun to make changes but there was still a financial crisis in Poland. To purchase anything, you needed government-issued coupons. The coupon program was theoretically initiated to eliminate shortages. However, since the shortages were real, not driven by over demand, the coupon program did nothing to improve conditions. It merely systematized and underlined the lack of necessary goods.

You needed coupons to buy essentials such as food, socks, shoes, and more. For example, you would get a coupon for one pair of shoes for the year. To use the coupon, you would have to stand in line for hours. When you got to the front of the line they might be out of your size. What could you do? Take whatever you could get and hope someone in your family could wear them or that you would be able to sell them. It was a little different with appliances and furniture. No coupons were issued for these larger items. But you might stand in line for a week, trading places with family members for the opportunity to purchase a refrigerator. At the end of a week there might not be any refrigerators, only a washer, so you are faced with the decision to wait possibly another week or two or maybe decide to take the washer because eventually you might need it.

There was an American store called Pewex in Poland, which was run by the government. You had to have US dollars or German Marks to shop there. You could buy what were considered to be luxury goods, such as clothing and other specialty items from the West like Lego bricks and video players. Wrangler jeans were very popular. They sold brand-name cigarettes, such as Marlborough, and chocolates. Chocolate Kisses were my favorite. But you had to have a lot of money to be able to afford to change Polish zloty to dollars and shop there. Other things rarely available in the Poland of my youth were bananas and oranges. My brothers and I would look forward to getting oranges for Christmas.

As an adult, I wanted to rent an apartment, but I was put on a waiting list. I was told that it would take about ten years for an apartment to become available. If I had joined the communist party, I would have had priority status. A party member would probably get an apartment in a matter of months. But this was not an option I ever considered. My only choice for the next ten years was to live with my in-laws. There was virtually no chance to get a good job.

My grandfather was born in St. Louis, but my great-grandparents moved back to Poland when he was just a child. My grandfather always said he wanted to return to the United States. He felt like an American and, actually, he was one, even though he had been taken back to Poland as a child. When he did finally move back in his late fifties, he took most of his family with him, my two aunts and my uncle. However, my mother was the oldest and decided to stay in Poland. She had already established her own family there. But because my grandparents were in the States, they were able to send money back to my mother.

The money they sent allowed my family to buy a used car and, since I was the only one in the family who knew how to drive, the car became mine and I used it to start a new venture as a taxi driver. It was independent work that allowed me to earn the most money in the shortest amount of time. Eventually, I saved enough of my earnings to buy a ticket to the United States.

Pitching

Pitching is a part of the game that is used within about sixty yards or less of the green. A general definition of pitching is that the ball is in the air for a longer distance than it rolls on the green. Every club in your bag is designed for a full swing. The 60-degree wedge is designed to reach between seventy to one hundred yards with a full swing, depending on the player's ability. How do you deal with a distance of forty or fifty yards before the green, either on the fairway or in the rough? In this situation you need to be ready to pitch.

The wedge is the shortest club in the bag. You use a wedge to pitch. There are several different wedges you can use from 48 degrees to 64 degrees. The difference in the loft of the wedges is what makes the difference in the trajectory of ball flight. There should be about 4 to 5 degrees difference between each of the wedges in your bag. For every 4 or 5 degrees, the difference will be about ten to twelve yards in distance. The lower the loft of the wedge, the lower the ball flight will be and the farther it will roll. Understanding how far your swing will take the ball using any given wedge comes simply with practice and experience.

Some instructors use a pitching method referred to as the "clock" method. Using this technique, you learn to visualize a clock as a reference tool. For example, when your shaft is at the nine o' clock position on your backswing your ball will travel about thirty to forty yards. At the ten o'clock position the ball may travel between forty and fifty yards. However, this all depends on the skill and speed of the golfer.

I do not believe this method is adequate to develop a reliable pitching stroke. The problem is that when you vary the length of your backswing, the different lengths will create a different feeling in the rotation of your body and can lead to using your hands and hitting "thin" or decelerating and being unable to control the distance.

As an example, at a recent member/member tournament at my club there was a playoff using alternate shots. The two favorites to win were long hitters. On the first playoff hole their tee shot reached a distance of 280 yards. The second player had only sixty yards remaining to make the green. Now he was suddenly faced with the need to hit a short distance. For him, that is about half of his full swing. Taking your swing down by 50 percent requires a lot of feel to create the shot and be accurate. He would probably reach at least 110 yards with his full swing using the shortest club.

He was afraid he would hit too far over the green. He tried to hit a soft shot and unintentionally decelerated. When you decelerate, the club is going faster than your hands so it creates a higher loft and falls short of the desired distance. His partner ended up in a difficult position. They finished with a bogey and were eliminated from the tournament. This is exactly why I teach my students to use a full swing but change the speed. Distance control is more efficient when regulating the speed of your swing.

In my teaching, I try to keep everything as consistent and simple as possible. With consistency comes greater odds of making the distance you require to end up as close as possible to the hole. I recommend using the feeling of the full swing and varying the speed of the downswing. The faster you hit, the higher and farther the ball will go. I would rather use a full swing and control the speed than attempt to control the length of the backswing.

My "path to golf" method of teaching is always to simplify the golfer's swing and make the swing as consistent and repeatable in any situation as possible. The only exception to my consistent, same grip, same full swing rule is when it comes to chipping or putting. In general, I recommend using the same setup, grip, and swing for any club. Keeping it simple is always best.

When you want to control the speed of your pitch using a full swing, the ratio between the backswing and the downswing remains the same, on average 3:1. This means three measures on the backswing and one to the moment of impact. Speed and tempo are two different things. Speed measures the start-to-finish timing, while tempo indicates the ratio of backswing to impact. You can have a successful outcome with a slow swing or a fast swing, but the tempo must remain constant. Some PGA tour players like Web Simpson have a very fast backswing and downswing. On the other hand, Ernie Els has a swing that looks very slow and in control. However, both of these professionals maintain a similar ratio between the backswing versus the downswing.

Lack of synchronization of the body with the correct tempo many times leads to a slice or hitting "fat." But, if the tempo is right, you will be noticeably more accurate and have better distance control. Tour tempo is a count of one, two, three to top, and one down to the moment of impact. The problem with this kind of count is that it is difficult to know exactly where you should be on the one or the two, so many people are confused. I use the same tempo, but I count it differently to avoid confusion. I begin by saying "and" as I start my backswing. Then count one is at the top and count two is the moment of impact. You will find out what your exact timing should be (faster or slower) through practice, while using the correct ratio (tempo).

.

CHAPTER 8

FULL SWING

Too Much Is Too Much

"The golf swing is like a suitcase into which we are trying to pack one too many things."
  -John Updike

"You know what they say about big hitters...the woods are full of them."
  – Jimmy Demaret

Once upon a time there was an occasional drip coming from the faucet of the tub in my upstairs bathroom. My wife, being the environmentalist she is, told me I should fix it. We were wasting water.

So, one Sunday I started out to do just that. Of course, I was careful to first close the shut-off valve in our basement. Then, I went upstairs and began disconnecting the faucet. Water rushed out as if from a firehose with such force it pushed me back. I grabbed a bath towel and held it against the force of the water. I called my wife to hold back the tide while I checked in the basement to determine the cause of the problem. But the force of the water was so strong she could not hold it and it pushed her to the opposite wall from the tub.

Our house was older, built around the early 1940s. Apparently, the shut-off valve had long ago rusted away. Where was the shut-off valve at the street? I couldn't find it. It was buried under years of soil and overgrown grass. We called the water company and got the emergency line. We were advised to leave a message. I called our plumber, no answer. We called half the plumbers we could find in the phonebook. No one answered, of course, it was Sunday.

I had visions of our home being swept down the street in a tidal wave caused by my faulty plumbing, water streaming into my neighbors' yards. What would happen if the water just kept blasting out at this rate? We called the fire department. They roared up the street with sirens blasting but they could not stop the water.

One thing the fire department was able to do was to get the water company on the phone. The water company then quickly sent a worker who had access to a diagram of the street. This allowed him to locate and access the water shut-off at the street. Finally, the water was stopped. Then one of the firemen gave us the phone number of a friend of his who happened to be a plumber. If we had not been able to get a plumber, we would have been without water until someone could install a properly functioning shut-off in the house.

This fiasco began at nine o' clock in the morning. By six o' clock that evening, my wife and I were sitting on the stairs leading down from the second floor. We were exhausted and frazzled and she looked over at me and said, "Well, we stopped the drip!"

The Full Swing

The moral of this story is that too much force is never a good thing. Especially not in golf. There are three main issues that will ruin a full swing every time. The first is an improper grip, one that does not fit your body. I covered this topic in Chapter 2. The second mistake is using too much force. The third is a bad takeaway.

It is natural for golfers to try to get more distance by hitting harder. Nearly everyone does it. Tell a golfer to try to hit farther and they will inevitably hit much harder. This problem should be easily fixed, and it is, if you let yourself. I think it is mostly psychological. The goal is to hit farther, but the brain translates this into "hit harder."

So, while forcing or overpowering a shot is a natural response, it will not achieve the desired outcome. This is the opposite of what you should be doing. The additional force you put into a golf swing tends to cause you to use your arms. Using your arms results in a sort of throwing motion, in other words, it is as if you are throwing the club toward the ball.

You forget to rotate your body so instead of your arms and hands following the rotation of your body as they should, your arms and hands are leading. As soon as your hands pass your center (your naval), you will be pulled forward and lose your balance.

Power in the golf swing comes from speed in the rotational movement of your body. It does not come from overpowering the swing. There is little hope for the average player to recover well from a serious mishit caused by using too much force.

A good example of this mistake took place at the 2022 PGA Championship when the winner, Justin Thomas, obviously an excellent player, shanked badly on the sixth hole of the final round. He was trying to hit harder than he normally would and it cost him. His ball went nearly 45 degrees to the right. But being the professional that he is, Justin was able to recover. He turned a bad shot into a bogey, just one over par and went on to win the tournament.

The third mistake is a bad takeaway. The takeaway begins with the head of the club at the ball and follows the path of the club from the ball to the top of the backswing. Two examples of professional players who use the "wrong" takeaway are Jim Furyk and Matt Wolf. Again, they are both excellent golfers. It took them years of practice to perfect the right movement using this type of takeaway. They both use a complicated movement called "looping." They disconnect their arms from their chest, going to the vertical position with the club and then looping back. The average golfer will find it nearly impossible to replicate this motion and to keep it consistent. Unless you are a full-time golf professional there just are not enough hours in the day to perfect this kind of swing.

To be consistent with your golf swing you must be in the same place every time on the top of your backswing. To do this you need good body connection. This means your arms are tight against the sides of your chest. It is much easier to achieve accuracy if you keep your arms against your sides. This stabilizes your swing and leaves less room for error. You also need to engage your core. Your swing is correct when the action is that of a pendulum. For the right-handed player, the left arm is straight all the way to the moment of impact.

Now that you understand what makes a bad swing, here are the three secrets of a good swing. Number one is always using your proper grip as explained in Chapter 2. The second is timing.

The PGA conducted extensive research concerning the ideal tempo of the full swing using both PGA and LPGA Professionals. The findings were quite consistent. As mentioned earlier a 3:1 tempo produces the best results. It means that the backswing should take three beats and the downswing should take one beat. Stated another way the backswing should take three times as long as the downswing. This holds true for nearly all players. It helps to actually count the timing in your head.

The third secret is balance, a very important factor in creating a great swing. Balance is initially established during your setup. Having the right shoes and even doing exercises designed to improve balance can help. But starting with good balance does not guarantee you will maintain it. The biggest culprit causing loss of balance is standing at an improper distance from the ball. Also, as mentioned earlier, leading with your arms during the swing will tend to pull you forward, thus causing you to be off balance. Check your backswing, if the plane of your swing puts the club head too far forward or backward at the top of the swing, this will pull you off as well. The bottom line is fast, well-timed rotation from a backswing that always ends in the same position equals a great swing.

CHAPTER 9

SPECIALTY SHOTS

When It Rains...

"Reverse every natural instinct and do the opposite of what you are inclined to do, and you will probably come very close to having a perfect golf swing."
  -Ben Hogan

There is something about the obstacles that you conquer that make you stronger. You learn to persevere. You learn that you can overcome more than you thought you could. Sometimes you find that you need to take a completely different approach, maybe even the opposite of what you had originally thought you should do. Specialty shots are the "difficult times" in life, in a golf game they can often be a time when you need to take an opposite approach. Just like difficult times, specialty shots require a lot of work, patience, perseverance, and maybe even a little faith that you can succeed.

Before I explain how you can improve your specialty shots, I'll share a couple of the challenging times I have experienced during my golfing career. Specifically, while I was working to meet one of the PGA requirements called the Playing Ability Test (PAT). The PAT is a nerve-racking thirty-six holes that must be played in one day with a prescribed outcome that depends on the course you are playing, and that needs to be passed to begin the program.

According to the PGA, less than 20 percent of those who participate in the PAT pass on any given try. As barriers to entry go, while it is not a perfect comparison, about 41 percent of those who apply to medical school are accepted and, while it varies state to state, upward of 70 percent of those who take the bar exam to become an attorney eventually pass. It takes an average of about five attempts to pass the PGA PAT and 50 percent of those who attempt it never pass. So, the barrier to entry is quite high. That may explain why there are only about 29,000 PGA members in the United States today. And let's just say that starting later in life and being self-taught, I was not part of the 20 percent who passed on my first time around.

One time, I was scheduled to play in a PAT. In the morning there was a light rain. But having driven the night before for four hours and stayed overnight in order to be on time, I was hoping the PAT would not be canceled. All I will say is, be careful what you wish for; the officials judged the course was playable and they wanted to proceed. There was no standing water on the greens, so that was good enough for them.

As the day went on, it continued to rain harder and harder. The rain was beating down on me and I could feel it seeping into my shoes. The wind was too strong to use an umbrella and it drove the rain straight at me and down the back of my shirt. The waterproof golf hat I was wearing did not cover my collar. The longer I played, the more water ran down my back. I began to wish the PAT had been canceled.

The rain forces you to make some fairly major adjustments. Because the ground is soft, the ball does not roll, and when it lands it usually just stops. On any other day, the ball would have rolled for a predictable distance, but in the rain, it was very difficult to judge how far it would go. When the odds are high, no matter what is happening, you just need to keep going. When I finished at the end of thirty-six holes, I had to dump water out of my shoes and literally wring out my clothing before I could drive home. In addition to practicing in wet conditions, I learned something valuable. Since that day, I always keep a waterproof hat that goes over the collar, a rain jacket, rain pants, and even waterproof socks in my car.

Another time I was playing early on a cold April morning. The temperature during the day was supposed to be in the midforties, but as I started to play, I could see there was some ice forming on a small puddle. On one of the par 3s my ball bounced off the green like it had hit concrete. It had hit frozen ground. The ball tore past the hole by about twenty-five yards. I had to pitch as softly as I could, hoping it would not roll off the hardened green. But it did roll off, forcing me to chip, and then it took two putts. Sadly, I double bogeyed that hole.

On another hole, I hit the ball off the tee and it was so cold the ball split in half. Half the ball went left while the other half went right. I guess it would have been a nice straight shot if the ball had remained intact. But half a ball is the true definition of an unplayable ball. I had to re-tee a new ball, and it counted against me. No one I talked to that day or since had ever seen anything like it.

At another tryout, I was on a par 5 using a driver. I thought my swing was pretty good, but the ball sliced out of bounds. According to the rules, I lost a stroke and distance, so I had to re-tee and count it as the third shot. The same thing happened on my next shot. I still thought my swing was decent. I lost a stroke and distance again. I was teeing off again and it was my fifth stroke. This time I decided to use my 3-wood and I found the center of the fairway. I played the rest of the hole without any surprises and finished with a triple bogey or 3 over. But on the next hole I needed to use a driver. I could feel that the head of the driver was moving. At first, I thought the head might be disconnecting, but it was still well attached. Then I discovered the problem. The shaft of the driver was cracked. I could not use the driver for the rest of the PAT. This happened on the second hole of the first round I had to play that day. I ended up playing the rest of a thirty-six-hole tournament without a driver. It was an absolute disaster.

Bad luck, bad weather, and bad shots can all put your ball in places you did not intend. In these instances, you will often need to use a specialty shot to get out of trouble. I will explain these next.

Specialty Shots

Playing on the golf course, especially around the green, can require a lot of specialty shots. In this chapter I discuss nine specialty shots: hitting low, hitting high, uphill and downhill lies, sidehill lies with the ball below or above your feet, intentional hooks, intentional slices, and sand shots. When you are hitting toward the hill and your lead foot (the foot closest to the hole) is higher than your trailing foot, it's an uphill lie. A downhill lie is the opposite. Here you are hitting downhill. The other shots are self-explanatory. Chipping and pitching are covered in other chapters. Specialty shots require a lot of work but since your short game accounts for about 60 percent of your score, they are the way to dramatically change the outcome of your game.

Hitting Low

There are a number of reasons you might want to keep the ball low. A strong wind would be one reason. An obstacle such as a low-hanging tree branch is another. To execute this type of shot, you place the ball on the target line but closer to your trailing foot. By placing the ball in this way, the moment of impact will create less loft. But keep in mind that your ball will roll farther.

Another way to hit lower is to place the ball in the center of the stance and use a less lofted club. Using this method, you will need to shorten your grip by sliding down on the grip. Be sure to pay attention to your distance control. The longer the distance, the longer the club you need to use.

Hitting High

For any regular full swing, you should use about 80 percent of your full power. This is true for all clubs. Less than full power works better to maintain the correct timing and sequencing of the swing. But when a shot requires you to hit higher, you need to use 100 percent of your power to get the ball up and over the obstacle.

Another method you can use to hit high around the green is to open your stance and open the face of the club. Opening the face means turning the club slightly to the right for right-handed golfers. This will naturally increase the loft and the ball will go higher. When the ball lands, it will travel for a shorter distance. For example, when you are hitting over water or a greenside bunker and the flag is close by, the ball will go higher and stop sooner. You will create more backspin which creates less roll.

Uphill Lies

With uphill lies in general, the ball will tend to go slightly to the left for right-handed golfers. As long as you can remain in balance and keep both legs straight, you can hit the ball just like any other shot because the lowest part of the swing will be in the same place as any other shot. When the slope becomes so steep that it requires you to bend your uphill knee, you need to keep your balance on the lower part of the slope. You will need to adjust your shoulders so that they are parallel to the slope. From this position you will be unable to make a full swing because your position does not allow you to. Typically, you will not need to hit a long shot because an uphill lie usually is a short shot near the green or coming back to the fairway in order to avoid trouble.

Downhill Lies

For a downhill lie, do the opposite of the uphill lie. The ball will tend to go slightly to the right for a right-handed player. You will need to adjust for that. If you can keep both legs straight, you can hit the ball just like any other shot. If not, bend your uphill knee, then keep your weight on the leg that is on the lower part of the slope. You will need to adjust your shoulders so that they are parallel to the slope.

Sidehill Lies with Ball Below Feet

One of the most difficult shots is when the ball is below your feet. On sidehill lies, you can use two different methods of hitting. One is to use the club for the correct distance, but since the ball is below your feet at the moment of impact, the face of the club will be slightly open. In this case, take your stance facing to the left of your target. For right-handed gofers, the open face creates a slice, which takes the ball from left to right. The farther below your feet the ball is, the more you position yourself to the left.

The second method, which is the one I recommend, was best described by Ben Hogan in his book titled Power Golf. Take one club down, meaning more lofted. For example, instead of a 7-iron use an 8-iron and hit straight toward the target. Because if you hit a 7-iron and the ball is below your feet, the ball will go left to right, but if you use an 8-iron and set up straight, the ball will go straight. The bottom of the club will be nearly flat on the ground and therefore when you hit the ball it will eliminate the probability of a slice.

Sidehill Lies with Ball Above Feet

With the ball above your feet the face of your club will automatically be closed. That is to say, the face will point to the left. Take one club more for example, instead of an 8-iron use a 7-iron and shorten your grip. This is essentially the opposite of a sidehill lie with the ball below your feet as described above.

Intentional Slice

An intentional slice would be used on a dogleg right when there is an obstacle on the right that is too high to go over. I don't like to recommend changes to the swing even for specialty shots. I advise keeping your swing as constant and familiar as possible. Instead, I prefer to change the setup. For this type of shot you can set up the face of the club toward your target. Your target could be a landing area or a flag on the green, but you set your body facing to the left of the obstacle. With the face open, you will create a sidespin to the right and this will take the ball around the obstacle to the right toward your intended target.

Intentional Hook

An intentional hook would be used for a dogleg left when there is an obstacle on the left that is too high to go over. You point the face of your club toward the intended landing area, but your body is set up to the right side of the obstacle. Now when you swing, you will notice that the face of the club is naturally closed and this will create a side left spin that will go around the obstacle.

Sand Shots

When your ball is in the sand, it is the worst time to try to emulate PGA Professionals and tour players. They work on their game for hours and develop different ways of executing bunker shots. For the average player, these techniques will be virtually impossible to perform. Unless you plan to go pro, there just isn't enough time in the day to practice those shots.

My work-around for this is quite effective. Hit the ball like any other full shot from the fairway with one exception or trick. Dig your feet into the sand. This works for two reasons. For one you will get a better feel for the texture and density of the sand. The heavier the sand, the steeper the golf swing should be. The second reason, also the most important, is that using a full fairway swing you normally would hit the ball first and then the club goes into the ground to create a very small divot. But if you dig your feet into the sand, it will put you slightly below the level of the ball. That same fairway swing will hit the sand first. The lowest part of the swing will be in front of the ball and underneath the surface. Hitting the sand first in this way will force the ball up out of the sand.

CHAPTER 10

GOLF COURSE MANAGEMENT

Brains Beat Brawn

"Golf is 20 percent talent and 80 percent management."
-Ben Hogan.

One day I had the opportunity to work with a young player who was a long drive junior champion. I pointed out the direction and placement for the next shot that I knew would be the best layup on that hole. We were playing a par 4. The first thing he asked me was how far away the bunkers were. He was afraid he would hit so far that he would land in them. The shot was uphill. Considering the distance of about 310 yards and the wind in our faces, I did not think he would make it to the front of the bunkers where he wanted to lay up.

I recommended that he hit 240 yards for a comfortable shot and good placement. This would have set him up to make an easy par. I explained that trying to reach the front of the bunkers would not be the smart choice because it would restrict the second shot. There was a tree on the right side of the green which would be directly in the line of his next shot. However, he really wanted to prove that he could hit that far. His ego did not allow him to listen to my advice. As a result, he hit straight toward the bunkers but did not quite reach them. Though he hit an impressive 290 yards, it did not help him make par. On the next shot, the ball hit the tree and bounced off into the bunker. Because of this he was not close enough to the flag for one putt and ended with a bogey.

Using the advice I had given to him, I hit where I planned to and my second shot was on the green. I had two putts and ended up with a par. The moral of the story is that if you use golf course management correctly, you will be able to lower your score by several strokes. Don't be tempted to show how far you can hit.

Another example of ego getting in the way of good golf course management can be seen in the movie Tin Cup, which was based on a true story. The movie was filmed at Deerwood Country Club, northeast of Houston, Texas. In the movie, a has-been golf pro named McAvoy, currently running a nearly bankrupt driving range, decides to prove to himself and his new love interest that he still "has it" by winning the US Open. He qualifies and, despite a few foibles, is well on his way to winning. But his ego gets the best of him on the final hole. In the movie, it was supposed to take place on the eighteenth hole of the US Open, which was a par 5. However, the scene was actually filmed on the fourth hole at Deerwood, a par 4.

There is a water hazard and, despite good advice from his caddie to lay up, he tries to go over the water. A birdie would win the tournament, a par would force a play-off. But McAvoy insisted on throwing it all away, taking a heartbreaking twelve strokes to pass the water. If you haven't seen the movie, I recommend you do.

I heard a story about Ben Hogan from an honorary member of the golf club where I work. He was a very successful amateur player and years ago he found himself playing in a group one hole behind Hogan. As a young player, this member was interested in observing Hogan and trying to understand how high-level players approach the game. On one par 5 in particular, Hogan could have reached the green in two but instead he laid up. His next shot was placed close to the hole, and with one putt he made a birdie. After the round the member walked up to Hogan and asked, "Mr. Hogan you could have reached the green in two shots, why didn't you go for it?" And Hogan's simple answer was, "Did I have to?" Hogan was most concerned about setting up for the next shot rather than risking a long or difficult shot that might put him in a bad position. This was one of Ben Hogan's greatest strengths, good golf course management. While he was arguably one of the best strikers in history, he never had a hole in one. If you want to play well, don't play to impress people. Instead, play for a good score, whether you play professionally or just for enjoyment.

Golf Course Management

With proper golf course management, the average golfer can shave about four or five stokes per round off his/her total score, so take advantage of this. It will make a difference at the end of the day.

As much as accuracy and distance are important, it is equally important to plan a strategy. The strategy starts on the tee box. If there is a hazard on the right side of the fairway, you should place the ball closer to the right tee marker for either left- or right-handed players. This creates a better visual angle toward your landing area. For example, if water is on the right side and you start from the right side of the tee box, the angle of your shot will be toward the center of the fairway, and thus away from the hazard. But if you set up on the left side, the line toward the center of the fairway will be angled toward the right and toward the hazard. Because of this you have more probability of ending up in the hazard.

Make sure you know the yardage that you can hit with each club. Not only the carry distance but the total distance, which means the carry distance plus the rolling distance. It is not always worth using a driver from the tee if there are hazards in front of you. You might want to take a shorter layup position.

Always think about the next shot and where you will be able to go from there. If you are on a par 4, you need to be on the green by your second stroke. This is known as a green in regulation (GIR). If it is a par 5, think about how far you can hit. You need to be on the green in three strokes. Many people try to get there in two and this frequently puts them into trouble.

You should not use the driver blindly. For example, if you are teeing up and you have 330 yards to the green, you might want to use a 3-wood. In this scenario, you would hit between 200 and 230 yards. Your next shot would be only 100 to 130 yards. This strategy is a much safer bet than trying to overpower the driver. Always choose a distance so that the next shot you take will be comfortable. Two comfortable shots making a GIR without stress is always the way to go. Then look at the pin position. If there is a hazard on the right, go to the left, and conversely if there is a hazard on the left, go to the right. If there is a dogleg or a sharp turn either to the right or the left, try to choose a club that allows you to reach the corner and lay up there. Many times, the best shot is not the longest shot. You should not try to compete with your playing partners for distance. Remember to always use your own strengths and don't risk too much.

When you try to hit harder to make the extra distance, it throws off your timing and your balance. Your body will not be synchronized through your swing. In other words, you may have a tendency to let your hands lead or rotate your hips early. You may take too long of a backswing and then you will be unable to continue the rotation of the downswing. In this case, at the moment of impact the club face will be closed, creating a hook. If you have a shorter backswing but try to hit faster, the early hip rotation will create a slice. Either way it won't work out well. Always choose the next club, the club that allows you to easily make the distance. For example, instead of a 6-iron, use a 5-iron.

For good golf course management, you need the right clubs for distance control. A set of clubs is designed so that the loft between each club is about 4 to 5 degrees. This difference in degree of loft gives you about ten to twelve yards in distance. Make sure to avoid gaps in the distance your clubs can reach. For example, if you can reach 110 yards with a pitching wedge and you can reach 130 yards with your next club, which is a 9-iron, you have at least an eight- to ten-yard gap. Getting 110 from your pitching wedge your next club should give you 120 to 122. Instead, you can reach 130, leaving a gap in yardage. Any PGA Professional in your area can adjust this for you by adjusting the loft of your club.

Players who have a low trajectory can control the distance of ball flight, but once it hits the ground it is difficult to judge how far it will roll. Again, it's like water coming out of a hose.

If you direct the stream of water low, it will splash and continue to run. If you direct the water too high, it goes into the air and lands without splashing much. With a golf shot that is too high you will have limited roll. To find out how far you hit with each club and how far it will roll, look for a golf facility that can measure your distance for you. The bad news is that once you understand your total distance for each club on a flat surface, only practice and experience will allow you to know your total distance on different terrains.

As you can see from the information I've shared above, golf course management is important and complex. But the more you avoid water, bunkers, and other hazards, the better your game will be and the more enjoyment you will have.

CHAPTER 11

KEEPING WHAT YOU LEARNED

PGA Professional, How Hard Could It Be?

"Golf is a science, the study of a lifetime, in which you can exhaust yourself but never your subject."
– David Forgan

Most people have no idea what it takes to become a PGA Professional. They tend to think that you have to play golf well and maybe that you have studied the rules of golf a little more closely than the average golfer. But becoming a PGA member and earning the right to use the logo is much more challenging than that. It takes longer than most master's degrees to complete, and in addition to coursework and exams there is that grueling thirty-six-hole Play Ability Test (PAT).

Before you can even begin the PGA program there are hoops to jump through. There is a background check and a qualifying written test. In order to take the qualifying test you must first purchase the materials for and pass five entry courses, which are: Introduction to the Professional Golf Management (PGM), Introduction to the Golf Profession, PGA History, PGA Constitution and By-laws, Rules of Golf and Career Enhancement. The test is administered at a third-party testing site. All the above mentioned will qualify you to enter the first level, the PGA Affiliates level.

If you make it to the affiliate level, you have begun the program. You have three levels to go through before becoming a PGA Professional. Each level consists of about ten subjects, and at the end of each level there is a final exam administered at a testing center on each of the subjects in your level.

The courses you need to take are not limited to those dealing with the field of golf. There are courses in business, accounting, finance, and marketing. You also need to take a course in basic anatomy, retailing, restaurant management, and human resources. In addition, you need to learn how to teach golf at all levels from beginners to low handicappers. You learn a lot about golf course maintenance, turf and grass, and golf course design as well. Each level has specific courses that need to be taken.

When you get to the second level, you are now considered an associate. At this point you must be employed full-time in a job that is related to golf and fits one of the PGA-approved employment classifications.

Before you begin the third level, you must pass the PAT. There is a list of assigned golf courses to choose from. You will need to pay the travel expenses and registration fees out of your own pocket. The total score you must achieve from both rounds depends on the rating of the golf course. However, on average you must score in the mid-70s without using a handicap. The pressure of thirty-six holes played on the same day, with the score determining your future career and livelihood, is considerable. It is enough to intimidate many entrants to play worse than their average game.

The full program is planned for about three years per level or nine years total. But since the courses are self-study you can progress at your own speed. It is generally thought that this program can be completed in about three to five years if you work at it diligently. On the other hand, if all the requirements are not completed within nine years, you are out of the program and would need to start all over again.

Once this herculean task is accomplished and you have passed the third level, you can begin your career as a PGA Professional. For me this meant typically working eleven to thirteen hours a day, six days a week. If there is a special outing, we will work thirteen days straight. I do whatever is necessary, from teaching and manning the golf shop even to cleaning golf carts and blowing leaves. There is a perception that PGA Professionals can play golf all day, which at least in my experience has not been the case, and from what I understand is not the case for most PGA members. But I will say, now that I am specialized in teaching and coaching, I teach and play much more than in the past. And one of the great perks of working in the Northeast is that I have the winter off.

Keeping What You Learned

I recommend taking lessons from a PGA Professional at least at certain points during your development; getting a good start, getting a tweak when things are not going well and even in some cases, but few, rebuilding your swing from scratch and starting again. An instructor can start you on your path. He/she can fast-track your progress. However, the tips that I have given you will help you to view your progress differently and will be of great assistance to you in understanding what your instructor is asking you to do. The information I share in this book may even help you to pick the right instructor and realistically judge your progress rather than allowing yourself to stay trapped at one level or, worse yet, going backward.

When people first begin playing golf, as with anything in life, they are often enthusiastic about working on their game and trying to improve. As the years go by, we get stuck in patterns. Often, we don't realize that something has changed or is just a little off. Many changes occur that may disrupt your game, including changes in your posture, strength, and flexibility. Other disruptors could be injuries you may have experienced, and even new or worn equipment. You need to adapt and change to keep playing the way you would like to play. And it is possible to keep improving even later in life, but it takes work and strong will.

Beware that your grip will change if your posture changes. But this can be corrected by reevaluating and modifying your grip (refer to Chapter 2). Distance will change with flexibility, and a fix for this can be a club fitting that may help you to achieve better results.

In addition to conditions that affect your physical ability for better or for worse, there are also always updates in the information that is currently available. There is a lot of new scientific research about how ball flight is affected by rain, heat, humidity, and by side spins. Who knows what we will learn in the future? So, even if your body condition has not changed, it is a good idea to look into new theories that exist on how to best improve your game. New information provides new opportunities to learn that should be taken into consideration.

In the end, to be successful in golf there are no shortcuts. You need to work on your game. Consider the fact that about 60 percent of your score comes from the short game (e.g., chipping, pitching, and putting, bunkers and special shots). You can improve your game a lot by working on the short game instead of using your driver on the range for an hour. Driving is important, but the most strokes you can eliminate from your score card come from around the green and from good golf course management.

While golf can be frustrating, the better you play the more enjoyable it is, especially when you see yourself improving. And I believe that if you are not going forward, you are probably falling back. The comfortable feel of the swing you have gotten used to and the reality of that swing can be two different things. So, think about your work on your game as an investment. Some practice and a tune-up lesson can go a long way. The return on investment will pay off in years of enjoyment.

Regardless of the difficulty, I love being a PGA Professional and I love the game of golf. I am one of those crazy types who is happy just smelling the freshly cut grass on the golf course. I honestly believe that golf is the greatest game. Golf is a truly individual sport.

You are competing only against yourself, the conditions, and the terrain in an attempt to be better today than you were yesterday. Every hole you play is different every time you play it. The two platitudes, "Nothing in life that is worth doing is easy" and "Anything that is worth doing is worth doing well," could not be truer than in the game of golf. As much as this challenging, complex, ever-changing game is an individual sport, we cannot deny the social benefits as well as the fact that it can be played outdoors in some of the most beautiful locations in the world. What more could you ask for? So, work on it and enjoy this wonderful game for life. And again, happy golfing!

GOLF CROSSWORD PUZZLE

From: Golf Crosswords for Adults, Clarity Media Courtesy of www.puzzle-book.co.uk - solution on next page

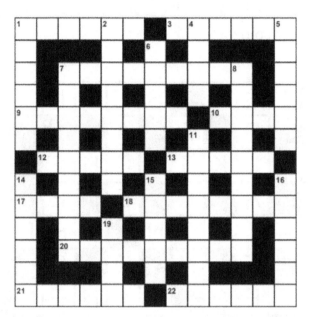

Across

1 Peter ___ : former golfer considered the 'voice of golf' (6)
3 Extracts a metal from its ore (6)
7 Golf competition for leading amateurs (6,3)
9 The flying of aircraft (8)
10 Greek god of war (4)
12 Clean with a brush (5)
13 Evergreen trees (5)
17 Transport device used to get around the course (4)
18 Michael ___ : New Zealand golfer who won the 2005 US Open (8)
20 This makes a golfer very happy, typically happening on a par three (4,2,3)
21 Up-to-date and fashionable (6)
22 Like a competition for golfers typically aged 50+ (6)

Down

1 Real; not virtual (6)
2 Scatter upon impact (8)
4 Spice made from nutmeg (4)
5 Most secure (6)
6 Criminal (5)
7 Kathy ___ : female golfer who won 88 times on the LPGA Tour (9)
8 Continue (9)
11 Show to be false (8)
14 Navigational instrument (6)
15 ___ Love III: US golfer who played in 6 Ryder Cups and has also captained the USA (5)
16 Gary ___ : South African golfer who won nine majors (6)
19 Lump of earth (4)

CROSSWORD PUZZLE SOLUTION

From: Golf Crosswords for Adults, Clarity Media Courtesy of www.puzzle-book.co.uk

About the Author

JERRY CHYLKOWSKI, PGA

Originally from Torun, Poland, Jerry has been a Connecticut resident since 1988. He is the teaching professional at the Connecticut Golf Club in Easton and lives in Fairfield County with his wife, Deborah. His love of golf, like his love for his wife, was sudden, spontaneous, and enduring. These two passions remain at the center of his life. Jerry holds the advanced PGA specialization in Teaching and Coaching, as well as in Executive Management. In 2010, he achieved a lifelong dream of becoming a US citizen. As a proficient ballroom dancer and DJ, he and his wife love to dance. Jerry often quips, "Golfing during the day and dancing at night; it's a pretty good life." When he is not golfing, he also enjoys travel, skiing, and family time with his grown stepson and stepdaughter.

www.onepathtogolf.com

If you like it, please do me the favor of reviewing it. As a reader, it is easy to forget how important reviews are to the author.

www.amazon.com/Forbidden-Golf-Communist-Poland-PGA-ebook/dp/B0BWLVZY9F

Acknowledgments

I have always considered myself to be a self-motivated and somewhat private person, particularly in my professional life. I tend to put my head down and work and learn independently. The writing of this book has been a completely different experience. So many facets of the process were new and unknown to me. I have to admit I depended on my wife for some help with the English language, which is her first and my third. In addition, many friends and colleagues helped in many ways. I would like to thank Lili Walker, Lesley Bannatyne and Brenda Puryear for initial editing and final editing by Kelli Larrubia and Elaini Caruso. The students who participated in my original data collection, Mike Bass, Steve Doubleday, Jerry Gregory, Jason Lucas, Ryan McNamara, and Paul Puryear. Denise Leidy for her suggestions regarding the title. Lisa Krasnow for the beautiful realization of my vision for the cover and David Emberling for the professional photos. Rod Loesch, the first Head Professional I worked for who believed in me and encouraged me to start the PGA program. Kevin Compare, Master Professional, and my PGA mentor whose help was invaluable to me in becoming a Specialized PGA Professional and was one of my first beta readers. And to all my students whose progress and praise gave me the confidence to move forward with this project.